GRACE
for YOU

GRACE
for YOU

A COMPELLING STORY *of*
GOD'S REDEMPTION

JOHN MACARTHUR

THOMAS NELSON
Since 1798

NASHVILLE DALLAS MEXICO CITY RIO DE JANEIRO BEIJING

Published in Nashville, Tennessee, by Thomas Nelson. Thomas
Nelson is a registered trademark of Thomas Nelson, Inc.

Published in association with the literary agency of Wolgemuth &
Associates, Inc.

Thomas Nelson, Inc., titles may be purchased in bulk for
educational, business, fund-raising, or sales promotional use. For
information, please e-mail SpecialMarkets@ThomasNelson.com.

Unless otherwise marked, Scripture quotations are taken from
the New King James Version. © 1982 by Thomas Nelson, Inc.
Used by permission. All rights reserved.

Scripture quotations marked NASB are taken from The New
American Standard Bible®, (NASB) © The Lockman Foundation
1960, 1962, 1963, 1968, 1971, 1972, 1973, 1975, 1977, 1995. Used by
permission.

The material in this booklet is adapted from *A Tale of Two Sons:
The Inside Story of a Father, His Sons, and a Shocking Murder.*

ISBN: 978-1-4002-0239-3

Printed in the United States of America

08 09 10 11 12 QW 9 8 7 6 5 4 3 2 1

GRACE *for* YOU

Stories about a maverick rabbi from the backwater village of Nazareth had been trickling south out of Galilee for months. Homes, marketplaces, and even the great temple in Jerusalem buzzed with talk of the man named Jesus and whether His miracles were genuine, fake, or conjured by the power of hell. Those who had seen Him in person said He could be none other than the Messiah. Only a powerful man of God could heal diseases, straighten deformed limbs, give sight to blind eyes, and open deaf ears. Some even said they had seen Him breathe life into dead bodies. So, when Jesus arrived in Jerusalem, news spread through the city like a choice bit of gossip and drew large crowds to wherever He happened to be.

On one particular occasion, the religious elite came to probe His theology, but were dismayed to find Him encircled by a large group of tax collectors and other people who had little interest in the temple. The experts in all things religious were even more distressed that Jesus appeared to *enjoy* the company of such spiritual undesirables. How could a genuine man of God be so undiscerning?

As the Pharisees and experts in Jewish

Scripture lurked on the fringes of the crowd and grumbled to one another, Jesus told a story.

A certain man had two sons. And the younger of them said to his father, "Father, give me the portion of goods that falls to me." So he divided to them his livelihood. And not many days after, the younger son gathered all together, journeyed to a far country, and there wasted his possessions with prodigal living. But when he had spent all, there arose a severe famine in that land, and he began to be in want. Then he went and joined himself to a citizen of that country, and he sent him into his fields to feed swine. And he would gladly have filled his stomach with the pods that the swine ate, and no one gave him anything.

But when he came to himself, he said, "How many of my father's hired servants have bread enough and to spare, and I perish with hunger! I will arise and go to my father, and will say to him, 'Father, I have sinned against heaven and before you, and I am no longer worthy to be called your son. Make me like one of your hired servants.'"

And he arose and came to his father. But when he was still a great way off, his father saw him and had compassion, and ran and fell on his neck and kissed him. And the son said to him, "Father, I have sinned against heaven and in your sight, and am no longer worthy to be called your son."

But the father said to his servants, "Bring out the best robe and put it on him, and put a ring on his hand and sandals on his feet. And bring the fatted calf here and kill it, and let us eat and be merry; for this my son was dead and is alive again; he was lost and is found." And they began to be merry.

Now his older son was in the field. And as he came and drew near to the house, he heard music and dancing. So he called one of the servants and asked what these things meant. And he said to him, "Your brother has come, and because he has received him safe and sound, your father has killed the fatted calf."

But he was angry and would not go in. Therefore his father came out and pleaded with him. So he answered and said to his father, "Lo, these many years I have been serving you; I never transgressed your commandment at any time; and yet you never gave me a young goat, that I might make merry with my friends. But as soon as this son of yours came, who has devoured your livelihood with harlots, you killed the fatted calf for him."

And he said to him, "Son, you are always with me, and all that I have is yours. It was right that we should make merry and be glad, for your brother was dead and is alive again, and was lost and is found."

(Luke 15:11–32)

Of all Jesus' stories, this one is the most richly detailed, powerfully dramatic, and intensely personal. It's full of emotion—ranging from sadness, to triumph, to a sense of shock, and finally to an unsettling wish for more closure. The characters are familiar, so it's easy for people to identify with the prodigal, to feel the father's grief, and yet still (in some degree) sympathize with the elder brother—all at the same time. The story is memorable on many levels, not the least of which is the gritty imagery Jesus invokes. The description of the prodigal as so desperately hungry he was willing to eat husks scavenged from swine food, for instance, graphically depicts his youthful dissolution in a way that was unspeakably revolting to His Jewish audience.

Another thing that makes this tale unforgettable is the poignancy demonstrated in the father's response when his lost son returns. The father's rejoicing was rich with tender compassion. Heartbroken and no doubt deeply wounded by his younger son's foolish rebellion, the father nevertheless expressed pure joy, unmingled with any hint of bitterness, when his wayward son came dragging home. Who would not be moved by that kind of love?

Few people, however, remember much about the elder son in the parable. His steely-hearted resentment over the father's mercy to his brother is often overlooked in many of the popular retellings. Nevertheless, it is the main reason Jesus told the parable. The parable of the prodigal son is not a warm and fuzzy feel-good message, but a powerful wake-up call with a very earnest warning for Pharisees (and all their spiritual cousins) about the deadly dangers of self-righteousness.

There's another good reason this short story captures the imaginations of so many hearers. We recognize ourselves in it. The parable reminds us of the most painful aspects of the human condition, and those who take an honest look will be able to identify with one aspect or another of the prodigal's experience. It is a moving story of repentance, forgiveness, redemption, and joy, touching our deepest human feelings.

Nevertheless, to understand the parable properly, we must see it through the eyes of someone in the culture of first-century Judaism. In such a context, the idea that God would freely accept and forgive repentant sinners (including the very worst of them) was a shocking and revolutionary concept. Almost no one in that society could conceive of God as reaching out to sinners. Most thought His only attitude toward sinners was stern disapproval. It was therefore the repentant sinner's duty to work hard to redeem himself and gain whatever degree of divine favor he could earn—mainly through long-term obedience to the ceremonial minutiae of Old Testament Law. That's why Jesus' practice of immediately receiving such people into His fellowship was such a public scandal.

While the religious experts lurked in the background, muttering propaganda among themselves, the rabble and riffraff of Jewish society drew closer to hear Jesus' story. I invite you now to pause what you're doing and to move in for a closer look at this familiar tale. I am confident you will find the time well spent. And, if you are willing, you may not ever be the same again.

Jesus began by introducing the main characters: "A certain man had two sons."

The Shameless Sinner

The picture Jesus paints is of a young man, who is apparently not yet married—because he wants to go and sow his wild oats. The word *prodigal* is a very old English word that speaks of reckless wastefulness or lavish extravagance. It is sometimes used in reference to wayward sons and daughters, but it doesn't speak of youthful rebellion per se. The main idea behind the word *prodigal* is that of wastefulness, immoderation, excess, and dissipation. But don't get the notion that the young man's dominant character flaw was merely that he was a spendthrift. Jesus used an expression for "prodigal living" that conveys strong overtones of licentiousness, promiscuity, and moral debauchery.

This restless son was probably in his teens and obviously filled with shameless disrespect toward his father. His request for an early inheritance reveals how passionately deep-seated and shamefully hard-hearted his defiance was. Anyone acquainted with Middle Eastern culture would instantly see this. For a son in that culture to request his inheritance early was tantamount to saying, "Dad, I wish you were dead. You are in the way of my plans. You are a barrier. I want my freedom. I want my fulfillment. And I want out of this family now. I have other plans that don't involve you; they don't involve this family; they don't involve this estate; they don't even involve this village. I want nothing to do with any of you. Give me my inheritance now, and I am out of here."

Incidentally, in that culture, the normal response to this level of impudence would be, at the very minimum, a hard slap across the face from the father. This would typically be done publicly to shame the son who had showed such disdain for his father. So a son guilty of dishonoring his father to this degree could well expect to be dispossessed of everything he had and then permanently dismissed from the family. Reckoned as dead. That's how serious this breach was. It was not uncommon in that time and place to hold an actual funeral for a child who insolently abandoned home and family in this way. Even today in strict Jewish families, parents will sometimes say "kaddish" (the formal recitation of a funeral prayer) over a son or daughter who is disowned for this kind of behavior.

Once disowned, there was almost no way for a rebellious child to come back and regain his position in the family. If wanted back at all, he must make restitution for whatever dishonor he had caused the family and for whatever possessions he might have taken when he ran away. Even then, he could expect to forfeit many of the rights that he previously enjoyed as a family member. He could certainly forget about receiving any further inheritance.

The young man came to his father demanding his share of the family belongings. He wanted an early inheritance. In order to fulfill this request, his father's household goods, personal valuables, and miscellaneous material possessions would have to be inventoried and distributed early. That suggestion was, of course, as impractical as it was audacious. In any two-son family following the normal customs of the day, one-third of all family assets would go to the younger son *when the father died.* To demand a third of the household goods while the father was still living was both absurd and unreasonable. The only workable solution was to estimate the fair market value for the family's belongings and issue most of it to the young man in cash. That is, of course, what he really wanted.

In the village life of that time, everyone knew everyone else's business. So, the prodigal's plan to leave home guaranteed that his rebellion would in short order become public knowledge and trust for the village rumor mill. This thoughtless rebel was blithely erecting a mountain of dishonor over his father, his family, and his own reputation.

Rather than publicly strike the boy across the face or disown him for his insolence, this father granted his rebel son exactly what he asked for. This sudden turn in Jesus' story would have elicited a second gasp from the scribes and Pharisees. To honor an impudent request from a defiant youth in this way was unheard-of. And by the standards of that culture, it was a pathetically weak response. The fact that the younger boy was free to take his father's bequest and go off into a far country suggests that there were no strings attached. The prodigal took his portion of the family wealth without looking back. He had exactly what he wanted: absolute freedom.

The phrase "gathered all together" means that the prodigal liquidated whatever he could, turning all his inheritance and possessions into ready cash. He then "journeyed to a far country," meaning, obviously, a Gentile country. This young man left not only his home and family but also his cultural heritage and his faith. He had so much scorn for his father that he deliberately exposed him to the most humiliating kind of public disgrace. That was bad enough. Add this boy's shallow materialism, his greed, his foolishness in forfeiting so much of the value of his heritage—and you already have a top-drawer delinquent. But when (on top of all that) the boy travels into a Gentile land to get as far away as he can from everyone who knew him—just so that he could indulge freely in evil behavior—he suddenly becomes such a hideously despicable figure that it would be hard to express his badness in mere words.

Surely Jesus was setting this guy up to be the main villain in the story. And the religious leaders must have wholeheartedly agreed.

Evidently, the prodigal wasn't interested in establishing a life of his own in a new place. He was simply looking for pleasure. And let's be honest: people who think like that typically don't think very far ahead. So it's no huge surprise when we read that he "wasted his possessions with prodigal living" (v. 13). He squandered a fortune in no time, spending his inheritance in the pursuit of vain pleasure. The clear impression from the Greek phrasing is that he pursued a lifestyle of utter dissipation and gross immorality that was far-flung and uninhibited by any kind of scruple.

Sin never delivers what it promises, and the pleasurable life sinners think they are pursuing always turns out to be precisely the opposite: a hard road that inevitably leads to ruin and the ultimate, literal dead end. Right after the money ran out, "there arose a severe famine in that land" (v. 14). The famine was not the prodigal's fault, of course, but that's how life is. His foolishness presumed upon a certain kind of future, and his rebellion against both his God and his father left him nowhere to turn to find relief.

Famines were common enough in Jesus' time that He did not have to explain the young man's dilemma. It would have been seen—especially by the scribes and Pharisees—as a stroke of divine chastisement. Eyewitness accounts of severe famines in ancient times are difficult to read. And almost all of them have several features in common. They describe how people are driven mad by hunger. Acts of cannibalism are common. Death from hunger is often so widespread and frequent that bodies must be collected and removed each day. People resort to eating things such as grass, shoe leather, rotten flesh, garbage, and excrement.

This had become the prodigal's world, a nightmarish horror. He had made numerous bad decisions for himself, but now the hand of divine providence had made his troubles more severe than he could have imagined.

Nevertheless, his resolve to follow his own path remained strong.

The tenacity of some sinners is impossible to explain rationally. Some people are so determined to have their own way that even when they are being force-fed the distasteful consequences of their transgressions, they still will not give up the pursuit. They might literally be sick to death of their sin's repercussions, and yet they will not give up the sin itself. Sin is a bondage they are powerless to break.

That was the case with the prodigal son. Destitute, hopeless, and with his life lying in ruins all around him, he still was not quite ready to go home. Going home, of course, would mean confessing that he had been wrong and foolish. It also meant facing the resentment of his brother, owning up to the grief and heartache he had caused his father, and inviting public shame on his own head. Above all, it would mean accepting responsibility, living under accountability, and submitting to authority—all of which he had fled in the first place. So, he did what a lot of people try to do before they truly hit bottom. He desperately attempted to concoct a scheme that would enable him to weather the crisis and perhaps avoid truly having to face his sin and own up fully to all the wrong he had done.

Here was his plan B: "He went and joined himself to a citizen of that country, and he sent him into his fields to feed swine" (v. 15).

This was no real employment at all. Swineherding paid next to nothing—not enough even to meet the immediate needs of the prodigal. Feeding pigs was also demeaning work. It was virtually the lowest possible chore in the whole hierarchy of labor. It requires no skill whatsoever, so this was a role often given to people who were mentally deficient, bereft of all social skills, or otherwise unfit for life in polite society.

For the young man, born under the law of Moses, this was an especially degrading turn of events. Pigs were considered ceremonially unclean animals. That meant any contact with the animals was considered spiritually defiling. Moreover, since it was forbidden to eat pork, to participate in raising hogs for human consumption was considered grossly immoral—especially in the eyes of the scribes and Pharisees. So the nature of the job alone was automatically enough to seal the prodigal son's status as a permanent, irredeemable outcast in Israel.

Even so, the young man's rebellious resolve was deeply set. He accepted the job and went to work. The citizen "sent him into his fields to feed swine." That means the prodigal took up permanent residence out in the harsh wilderness, living with the hogs. He became a full-time swineherd. Could it get any worse for the young man?

Yes, it could. And it did.

During the famine, as resources became even more scarce, the pigs had to subsist on a diet of "pods." These were carob pods; long string-bean-shaped seed pods that grew on scrubby, treelike bushes. The beans inside the pods were hard, and the pod shells were tough and leathery, virtually inedible for humans and frankly not all that nutritious even for livestock. Nevertheless, the prodigal watched the swine greedily devouring those carob pods, and he found himself earnestly longing to fill his own stomach with the swine food.

Even in that distant Gentile land where practically no one was constrained by any scruples about ceremonial uncleanness or terribly repulsed by the eating of pork, the prodigal's station in life was now such that he was deemed untouchable. "No one gave him anything" (v. 16).

As Jesus told this parable, He ascribed to the prodigal every kind of defilement, disgrace, and dishonor imaginable. Because of all the various ways this young rebel had defiled and disgraced himself, by the time Jesus got to this point in the tale, the prodigal son was (by the Pharisees' way of thinking) quite clearly an object worthy of more contempt than pity. He was so utterly covered with reproach and ill repute that they had no doubt completely written him off as irredeemable.

THE TRUTH ABOUT SIN

All sin involves precisely this kind of irrational rebellion against a loving heavenly Father. Sin's greatest evil lies not in the fact that it is a transgression of the Law—although it most certainly is that (1 John 3:4). But the real ugliness of sin stems from its nature as a personal affront to a good and gracious Lawgiver. Our sin is a calculated, deliberate violation of the relationship we have with our Creator. (You may not have consciously considered sin that way before, but it is nevertheless true, and every person's conscience affirms that reality. The secrets of our heart bear witness against us, and Romans 2:14–16 says even those secrets will one day be revealed and judged by God.)

When we sin, we show disdain for God's fatherly love as well as His holy authority. We spurn not merely His law, but also His very person. To sin is to deny God His place. It is an expression of hatred against God. It's tantamount to wishing He were dead. And since all sin has at its heart this element of contempt for God, even the smallest sin has enough evil to unleash an eternity full of mischief, misfortune, and misery.

Moreover, sin always bears evil fruit. We cannot take the good gifts God has surrounded us with, barter them away as if they were nothing, and then not expect to reap the consequences of spiritual poverty that are the inevitable result.

Here's a shocking reality: the prodigal son is not merely a picture of the worst of sinners; he is a symbol of every unredeemed sinner—alienated from God and without a hope in the world (Ephesians 2:12). He is a precise and living effigy of the entire human race—fallen, sinful, and rebellious. Worse yet, his character reflects not only the state of our fallen race as a whole but also the natural condition of every individual ever conceived by a human father since the fall of Adam. We all begin this life with our backs turned against God, desiring to flee far from Him, with no regard for His love, no appreciation of His generosity, and no respect for His honor.

In other words, we are *all* prodigal sons and daughters. Every one of us is guilty of self-indulgence, dissipation, and unrestrained longing for what we want above all else. We have been heedless to the consequences of sin and reckless in the pursuit of evil. Apart from God's restraining grace, every one of us would have long ago wasted our lives and squandered every blessing God has given us.

The end of this young man's journey in the pig field perfectly exemplifies the destruction and heartache to which sin inevitably leads. Here the foolish sinner has exhausted his best plan B and must realize that it never could have worked in the first place. We lack the ability to repair our own broken lives. We can't possibly atone for the sins we have committed, so we can't make our guilt go away. There is absolutely no earthly answer for such a dilemma. It will not be found in psychology, group therapy, or self-help—and it is certainly not found in drugs, alcohol, or any other form of escape. You can't get away from sin's consequences by moving to a new neighborhood, by marrying a new partner, or by otherwise running away. When all such attempts at evading sin's payday are finally exhausted, the sinner truly hits rock bottom.

THE TRUTH ABOUT REPENTANCE

Rock bottom was precisely where the prodigal son finally found himself. He was one of those fortunate sinners who "came to himself" (Luke 15:17) before reaping the full and final wages of sin after death. The phrase actually means that he came to the end of himself—or in the words of a different translation, "he came to his senses" (NASB).

Working in the fields with the pigs turned out providentially to the prodigal's benefit. He woke up to reality. In the solitude of the pig fields, he was forced to face what he had become, and that somehow jolted him out of utter insensibility. Suddenly, he began to think clearly. His first instinct upon regaining his senses was to plan how he might get back to his father and his home. For the first time in his life, the younger son was determined to walk away from his sin, plead for his father's forgiveness, and submit to his father's authority.

The prodigal son's decision was not merely a superficial ploy to regain his father's sympathy, or a quick-and-dirty scheme to recover the comforts of his old life. This was deep, heartfelt repentance, and we see its genuineness in every step of his planned return to the father's household.

The first significant step in the prodigal's return involved taking an honest look at his situation. That meant facing the ugly reality of what he had become, accepting responsibility for what he had done, owning up to the severity of his guilt, admitting his utter helplessness, and turning to someone who could truly help. Here, I am convinced, is where true repentance always begins: with an accurate assessment of one's own condition. When one fully comes to terms with the truth, there is no pretense of dignity and self-confidence. There is no defensiveness. And there is certainly no demand for one's rights or a sense of entitlement.

Prior to this, the prodigal had not shown a hint of respect, affection, or even simple appreciation for his father. Now he was forced to confess that he would be vastly better off at the lowest level of servitude under his own father than far away in the pig fields, reaping the bitter fruits of his "freedom" and literally facing death as a reward for his foolish pursuit of selfish pleasure. He was broken. He was alone. He was downcast. He was penitent. He believed in his father. And that is precisely what makes the difference between mere remorse and authentic, saving repentance. The prodigal's trust in his father's mercy drew him toward his father rather than sending him fleeing even farther away.

The Truth About Salvation

The scribes and Pharisees—the religious leaders of Jesus' day—surely expected the prodigal son's father to drop the hammer hard on the wayward youth. One thing they were certain of: there could be no *instant* forgiveness. Nor was the prodigal likely to merit *full* reconciliation with his father, ever. Surely he would have to take his medicine in full doses.

In that culture of honor, especially in a situation like this, it would be nothing extraordinary if the father simply refused to meet the boy face-to-face. In fact, even if the father were inclined to grant the penitent son an audience, it would be fairly typical to punish him first by making a public spectacle of his shame. For example, he might have the son sit outside the gate in public view for several

days, letting him soak up some of the dishonor he had brought upon his own family.
The boy would be completely exposed to the
elements—and worse, to the derision of
the whole community. After a few days of
humiliation, if the father did decide to grant
him an audience, and if he were willing to
extend a measure of mercy, the son would be
expected to bow low and kiss the father's
feet. No embrace. It would not even be right
for him to remain standing as he kissed his
father's hand.

Most likely, that's precisely the kind
of treatment the prodigal son expected.
But Jesus' parable suddenly took another
dramatic and unexpected turn. "When he
was still a great way off, his father saw him
and had compassion, and ran and fell on his
neck and kissed him" (Luke 15:20).

Obviously, the father had been watching

daily, heartbroken but hopeful, privately bearing the unspeakable pain of suffering love for his son. He surely knew that the kind of life his son was headed for would eventually end up the way it did. He desperately hoped the boy would survive and come back home.

The imagery of the father running to meet the prodigal son fills in the details of the big picture even more. In the context of that culture, the father's action of running to the boy and embracing him before he even came all the way home was seen as a shameful breach of decorum. For one thing, noblemen did not run. Running was for little boys and servants. Grown men of stature walked magisterially, with slow gait and deliberate steps. But the father gathered up the hem of his robe and took off in a most undignified manner.

When the father reached the wayward son, he couldn't contain his affection, and he didn't hesitate in granting forgiveness. He immediately embraced the prodigal. Jesus said the father "fell on his neck and kissed him." The verb tense means he kissed him repeatedly. He collapsed on the boy in a massive hug, buried his head in the neck of his son—stinking and dirty and unpresentable as he was—and welcomed him with a display of unbridled emotion.

The prodigal had come prepared to kiss his father's feet. Instead, the father was kissing the prodigal's pig-stinking head. And the young man never even got to the part of his rehearsed speech in which he would ask to become one of the hired servants. This may seem a subtle detail in the parable, but it made a not-so-subtle point for the Pharisees' benefit. There was no way they could have failed to notice that the boy had done nothing to atone for his own sin, and yet the father's foregiveness was full and lavish anyway, with nothing held back.

Doesn't common sense demand that sins be atoned for? Didn't God Himself say He will not justify the wicked (Exodus 23:7) and that He will by no means allow the guilty to go unpunished (Exodus 34:7)? Whatever happened to righteousness? What about the principles of divine justice?

It is quite true that sin *must* be atoned for. Don't imagine for a moment that when God forgives sin, He simply looks the other way and pretends the sin never occurred. However, no sinner can ever fully atone for his or her own sin, and that is why the Bible so frequently stresses the need for a substitute. The Old Testament illustrated the need and promised that God would provide a suitable sacrifice (Genesis 3:15; 22:7–8; Isaiah 53:1–12). The New Testament tells us about the fulfillment of that promise.

God became a man in the person of Jesus Christ, who became our substitute.

The wages of sin is death, but the gift of God is eternal life in Christ Jesus our Lord. (Romans 6:23)

Christ Jesus, who, being in the form of God, did not consider it robbery to be equal with God, but made Himself of no reputation, taking the form of a bondservant, and coming in the likeness of men. And being found in appearance as a man, He humbled Himself and became obedient to the point of death, even the death of the cross. (Philippians 2:5–8)

Christ has redeemed us from the curse of the law, having become a curse for us, for it is written, "Cursed is everyone who hangs on a tree." (Galatians 3:13).

For [God] made Him who knew no sin to be sin for us, that we might become the righteousness of God in Him. (2 Corinthians 5:21)

While each of us deserves to die for our sins and to spend eternity separated from God—an existence described by Jesus as unspeakably miserable (Matthew 13:41–50; Luke 16:23–24)—the Son of God endured the penalty of sin on our behalf. Because Jesus paid the penalty for sin as our substitute, our heavenly Father can offer us complete forgiveness for sin without setting aside justice or denying His own completely righteous nature.

COMPLETE RESTORATION

The stunned prodigal son must have felt his head spinning. After everything he had done—and everything sin had done to him—he would hardly be able to grasp what was happening. The villagers would like-wise be completely baffled by the father's be-havior. What was he doing? Unconcerned with his own reputation, the father began showering the prodigal son with honor after honor, staggeringly generous favors, which the boy by no means deserved.

Jesus mentioned three gifts the father

immediately gave his penitent son: a robe, a ring, and sandals. Everyone understood the implications of each gift. The shoes were an important gesture that signified the former rebel's full and immediate reinstatement as a privileged son. The robe given to the son was a courtesy reserved for an extremely prestigious visiting dignitary. The expression used in the original Greek text of Scripture literally means "first-ranking garment," and signified high honor. The ring was a signet, which served as a kind of notary seal. With a signet ring, the bearer could conduct official business on behalf of the family. With this ring, the father restored the prodigal's authority as a son.

Having crowned his repentant son with the highest honor and privilege, the prodigal's father called for the party to end all parties: "Bring the fatted calf here and kill it, and let us eat and be merry; for this my son was dead and is alive again; he was lost and is found" (Luke 15:23–24).

How wonderful it would have been if this had been the end of the story. But Jesus would again stun His audience with another shocking turn. Suddenly, the whole character of the story changes with the arrival of the elder son.

THE STATELY SINNER

Sinners come in two basic varieties. Some are straightforward and intrepid in their evildoing, and they don't really care who sees what they do. Invariably, their downfall is pride—the kind of pride that is seen in an undue love for oneself and uncontrollable lusts for self-indulgent pleasures.

At the other end of the spectrum are

secretive sinners, who prefer to sin when they think no one else is looking. They try to mask their more obvious sins in various ways—often with the pretense of religion. Their downfall is also pride, but it's the kind of pride that manifests itself in hypocrisy.

As this parable of Jesus continues, it becomes obvious that the second (and opposite) kind of sinner is epitomized by the elder brother. This young man is an emblem of all the seemingly honorable, superficially moral, or outwardly religious sinners— people just like the scribe and the Pharisees. Here is a sinner who thinks he can cloak his inner rebellion with outward righteousness.

The prodigal son's brother had been out in the field that day. He was most likely overseeing a crew of servants and ensuring the future prosperity of the estate. Therefore, he was unaware of the celebration that was already underway at this house, even though the whole village had been in a buzz about it for hours. When the elder son arrived home, the party was already in full swing. Musicians and dancers were already leading the festivities as the smell of cooked meat permeated the air. The fact that he had not been summoned immediately seems to be clear evidence that at least the father could see what was really in the elder brother's heart.

As the elder son approached the house, "he heard music and dancing." The elder brother's surprise is perfectly understandable; but his extreme indignation is not so easily excused. His reaction suggests that he assumed from the get-go that whatever news had provoked such delirious joy on the part of his father was going to be something he would resent. If this son's heart were right—if he had even an ounce of genuine love or authentic concern for anyone in his family besides himself—the text would say, "He ran to the house to see what all the joy was about." Then his father would have said, "Your brother's home," and they would have embraced and rejoiced together with tears.

But the elder son remained outside. He kept his distance from the celebration and *demanded* an explanation, not from his own father, but from someone who would be totally intimidated by him. The servant boy's answer implies that he expected the elder brother to welcome the good news: "Your brother has come, and because he has received him safe and sound, your father has killed the fatted calf" (v. 27). These details told the elder son all he needed to know. His father had not only received the prodigal despite the boy's shameful behavior, but their broken relationship had also been completely restored.

Don't miss the real reason for the elder brother's intense displeasure. His pouting fury was not so much aimed at his prodigal brother, but against his grace-oriented father. Not only was the younger brother not receiving just punishment for his sinful behavior and for disgracing the family, the father was spending resources that would rightfully belong to the elder brother after the father's death—in effect, diminishing the value of the "faithful" son's inheritance. This is our first clue that the elder son was secretly more of a rebel than the prodigal had ever been.

The elder son gives us a vivid depiction of how the outwardly righteous person sees things. He doesn't comprehend the idea that divine grace is sufficient to save sinners. He resents the mercy of immediate forgiveness. He has been laboring his entire life to be respectable and to gain God's favor. And yet some of the most debauched sinners imaginable find instant forgiveness and full fellowship with the Father as though no wrong had been committed.

Whether he was willing to admit it or not, the elder brother needed the father's forgiveness and mercy as much as the prodigal. Instead of resenting his father's kindness to his returning brother, this son should have been the most eager participant in the celebration because he, too, was in desperate need of that kind of mercy.

The rebellion long suppressed underneath the elder son's dutifully maintained decorum had now broken into the open. The father no doubt knew the truth hidden in his son's heart all along. Still, rather than scolding this son (or worse), the father dealt gently with him: "[He] came out and pleaded with him" (Luke 15:28). He actually walked away from the celebration and went outside, where the elder brother was pouting. He begged the elder brother to relent of his self-righteous indignation. With nothing but mercy, he reached out to the boy the same way he had reached out to the returning prodigal Son. But this son's response was markedly different.

Hypocrisy is a deadly disease. It secretly kills from the inside out. Deep beneath a carefully polished religious veneer, hidden from the eyes of all but God, it deludes and destroys, fooling every mortal observer, especially its victim. Religious people are too often infected with this disease of self-deception. They expertly lie to themselves, perhaps because the truth is too difficult to bear. Deep down, these law-abiding, often religious sinners know that no amount of goodness will ever be good enough, so they relentlessly pursue goodness and work ever more diligently to convince themselves and everyone else that it is. The self-delusion can be so powerful they even presume to hold God to their standard of "goodness," and even dare to question His righteousness when He forgives those less deserving!

These stately sinners need God's compassion as much as, if not more than, prodigal sinners. The open sin of the prodigal son eventually gave him no alternative but to face his need for grace. Not so for many fastidious churchgoers. Having never fled their Father's homestead and having never given full expression to their rebellion, they pack church pews, dutifully give every appearance of obedience, and expect the

Father to give them what they feel to be their rightful inheritance. For them, God's blessings are earned, God's forgiveness must be coaxed out of Him, the title "Child of God" belongs to the dutiful. But, like the elder son, they do not know their Father, or the truth about sin and righteousness, goodness and forgiveness.

Apart from God's grace, no one has power to do anything but sin. Even good deeds are sullied by self-interest and pride. So those who presume to earn God's favor by doing all the right things only deceive themselves and thereby condemn themselves. Their works may appear good on a superficial level. They may be very impressive from a merely human perspective. But the Bible is clear: all human works, religious deeds, and acts of righteousness done with the notion of gaining God's approval are nothing but filthy rags in His estimation (Isaiah 64:6). They are tainted by impure motives. They are done with a desire to earn what God has promised to give freely, which only breeds pride and nurtures hypocrisy.

Grace is the *only* hope for any sinner.

Note how the elder son behaved. He refused to refer to the younger son as "my brother." Instead, he called him "this son of yours"—and then he purposely brought up the sins of the prodigal and reviewed them all in living color—even though he knew very well that the father had already declared those sins forgiven.

It appears he purposely hauled out the most offensive sins and put those on the table first. He was naming sins for which, technically under the Mosaic principles of justice, death was deemed a just punishment (cf. Deuteronomy 21:18–21). It was his subtle way of stressing that the prodigal son *should* be dead and that he would frankly be happier if he were. This was an amazingly cold-hearted and wicked attack on a son he knew the father loved—before the elder son had even shown the courtesy of greeting his brother and giving him an opportunity to express his repentance personally.

But even in the wake of that verbal barrage of resentment, the father responded with tenderness and a soft answer. "Son, you are always with me, and all that I have is yours. It was right that we should make merry and be glad, for your brother was dead and is alive again, and was lost and is found" (Luke 15:31–32).

Sometimes it is easier to be patient with prodigals than it is with dutifully religious people. As a pastor, I think of that often.

Formerly down-and-out sinners who have been wonderfully and thoroughly converted are a true joy. They have no room for hypocrisy. They tend to be enthusiastic, eager to learn, full of gratitude, and zealous about bringing others to Christ. The people who tend to cause pastors the most grief almost always seem to be the people who grew up in church and learned early how to be hypocritical. The complainers, the critics, and the curmudgeons usually come from that group. It sometimes takes an extra measure of grace to respond rightly to them.

There is no sign the elder son responded to the gentle pleas of his father. By all appearances, his heart remained as cold as stone. So the father made one final plea, and it was a full reiteration of the main theme that dominated several of Jesus' parables: "It was right that we should make merry and be glad, for your brother was dead and is alive again, and was lost and is found" (v. 32). For the father, the celebration was not only a natural response, it was mandatory. It would have been wrong not to celebrate.

The unspoken implication should have touched the elder son's heart: "We will celebrate for you, too, if you come."

That is where Jesus' telling of the parable ended—outside the celebration, with no satisfying resolution to the story. The father's plea to the elder brother simply hung in the air, and the parable ended with a tender appeal for his repentance. That is because Jesus told the parable to highlight the fact that a divine entreaty had been extended to the Pharisees—and remains available to all others who *think* they are worthy of God's grace and favor.

Heaven resounds with music and dancing

over the return of each prodigal. And these sounds of celebration are your invitation to enter. If you remain outside, there can be only one reason. You are unwilling to admit that you—in your own unique way—are a prodigal too. Only after you have accepted the truth of your own moral poverty will you allow yourself to enter the celebration. Until then, you will remain outside, either hoping to earn God's praise or trying to convince Him that you *deserve* a party.

Dear reader, if you have not entered the celebration as a prodigal, please . . . come in!

If you would like to read more fascinating insights about one of Jesus' most profound parables and discover the shocking ending to the story of the prodigal, the father, and the elder brother, *A Tale of Two Sons* by Dr. John MacArthur is available at a bookstore near you.

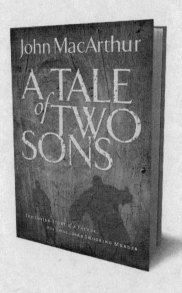

ISBN 978-0-7852-6268-8

Price $22.99